# Build the Perfect Team

# Build the Perfect Team

Robert E. Levasseur, Ph.D.

MindFire Press
St. Augustine, Florida

ISBN 978-0-9789930-7-8

Library of Congress Control Number 2021924379

Published by MindFire Press—St. Augustine, Florida

Cover Image: Cadillac Mountain South Ridge Trail, Acadia National Park, Mount Desert Island, Maine

I dedicate this book to the many mentors, colleagues, and students who shared their knowledge and insights about teams and what makes them work best; in particular, my wife, Donna Fox, a truly gifted organizational consultant.

# Contents

# Preface

Effective teams are critical to success in today's environment of rapid, technology-driven change. Hence, in this era of very high project failure rates,[1] it is not surprising that organizations search for ways to improve the performance of their teams. Google's intensive study of the characteristics of their best teams led them to an unexpected discovery.[2] The best teams create an environment of psychological safety by adopting two team norms that lead to important shared behaviors. Group development experts agree that psychological safety is essential to a high-performing team. However, as you will discover, building the perfect team involves more than setting team norms.

# The Perfect Team Model

# Chapter 1

## Balance the Team

If you want to build the perfect team, make sure the team has good balance. This means having people with relevant hard and soft skills, who think differently, are diverse and culturally aware, and understand the needs and capabilities of the people affected by the team's work.

### Hard and Soft Skills

To be successful, teams must include individuals with the hard and soft skills necessary to identify and develop effective solutions to the problems or opportunities they face. People with hard skills (such as technical and product knowledge), are easier to identify and add to the team than those with soft skills (such as self-awareness, communication, collaboration, and leadership). Potential team members as a rule have well-developed hard skills, typically gained through formal education or job-specific training. But most have inadequate soft skills because academic curricula do not stress the need for them and many leaders lack the time, knowledge, or ability to instill them. As team leader, you should include as members, whenever possible, people who bring both sets of skills to the team. When this is not possible, you should develop the soft (people) skills of those who lack them as part of the team development process, which you will learn how to do later, or through formal training.

## Different Ways of Thinking

Every team leader knows the importance of having people with the knowledge, skills, and experience needed to achieve the team's mission and goals. But many team leaders do not realize the importance of differing viewpoints to achieving those goals. Having the broad perspective that results when team members have different ways of thinking helps teams to avoid group think and improves the quality of the decisions they make as a team. But how do you as team leader ensure you have the right people with the right perspectives on your team?

One well-known, research-based method of understanding how people think is the Myers-Briggs Type Indicator (MBTI).[3] An MBTI type, as measured by answers to a scientific questionnaire, shows an individual's preference in each of four dimensions:

- Extroversion—Introversion (E/I)
- Sensing—iNtuition (S/N)
- Thinking—Feeling (T/F)
- Judging—Perceiving (J/P)

Extroverts focus outwardly; introverts focus inwardly. Sensing types rely on concrete data; intuitive types grasp the big picture without the need for much sensory data. Thinkers prefer to decide based on logic; feeling types make decisions based on their potential impact on people. Judging types are planners who seek closure; perceiving types are more spontaneous and prefer to leave their choices open. Opposites in each category balance out. Having team members who are similar along these four dimensions can lead to problems such as group think. Ensuring the team has members with different ways of thinking can help avoid this frequent problem. If you are interested, you can find out more about using MBTI to achieve team balance in Appendix A.

## Diversity and Cultural Awareness

Common sense suggests that the perfect team must consist of intelligent, knowledgeable, and motivated people. To avoid group think, having a blend of team members with hard and soft skills who look at problems differently is also important. In addition, having a diverse team increases the quality of decisions and the odds of implementation success even more because of the team's heightened ability to understand the culture into which their innovative solutions must fit. Team solutions to an organization's problems, regardless of how good they are technically, will not stick if they do not fit the culture.[4]

## User Perspective

To ensure they solve the real problem, the team needs to have a user perspective. The best way to do this is to include representatives of the user community on the team. The inclusion and active participation of people who will need to use the solutions developed by the team increases the odds of implementation success. As a wise business school professor of mine once said, "People support what they help to create."[5] This statement captures the essence of the change process—the best way to overcome resistance to change is to involve people affected by the change in the decision-making process as early and meaningfully as possible.

In the next chapter, we examine the findings of Google's research on the reasons for the high performance of their best teams.

# Chapter 2

## Create Psychological Safety

The second step in building the perfect team, and arguably the most important, is to set ground rules/norms that support the right team behaviors. Technically, you first set some ground rules for group behavior. They become norms when the team members adopt and consistently apply them to their common work. Foremost among these are norms to establish psychological safety.

### Psychological Safety

Think about how you feel when you meet a group of people for the first time. If you are like most people, you are more cautious than when you meet a few friends for lunch or a round of golf. Why? Because you feel safer when you are with friends. This is due to psychological safety. Based on research conducted by Google on their best teams, the most important action you can take to provide psychological safety is to create two team norms.[6] One norm will provide every team member with the opportunity to speak on issues discussed in team meetings. The second norm will encourage every team member to be sensitive to the needs and feelings of everyone on the team.

When building the perfect team, you must create a list of ground rules (expectations for individual behavior) for how team members will conduct themselves. And you must do this early in the team formation process and as a group to ensure the buy-in of all team members. While each team has to decide the precise wording of these desired team norms, you might state the ground rules for the two essential norms identified by Google like this:

- Give everyone a chance to speak during team discussions.
- Respect each other's needs and feelings.

The first norm provides the opportunity for, but does not force, each team member to speak. If someone has nothing to say on a topic, making them speak is not necessary to ensure their psychological safety and takes up valuable meeting time. Conversely, if someone has something to say, this norm ensures the team member has a chance to provide the benefit of their perspective to the team in a psychologically safe way. Most extroverts will want to speak first and, if allowed to by the leader, may use up the time allotted for discussion. The first norm ensures the team will hear the views of the introverts on the team when they are ready to speak, which is often later in the discussion. Letting each team member decide whether and when to speak creates a sense of inclusion (of being an integral part of the team).

The second norm, which is a powerful statement of the importance of each individual on the team, sets the tone for team meetings. This norm contrasts sharply with the implicit norm of meetings run by leaders in a top-down manner. In such meetings, the norm is that a person speaks only when directed to or, if bold enough to offer a contrary opinion, prepares for the criticism that too often results from saying something that the leader (or some other team member) does not agree with. Think of the chilling effect this lack of psychological safety has on team members. Effectively muzzled, is it any wonder most people feel traditional meetings are a waste of time or worse? Showing respect for each team member is not a luxury. Without it, you cannot build the perfect team!

## Engagement and Collaboration

People seek engagement in their work. Unfortunately, they seldom find it in today's work environment.[7] To build the perfect team, you must set norms that support the active engagement and collaboration of all members. A set of ground rules for this purpose, including the two described previously that support psychological safety, might include:

- Give everyone a chance to speak during team discussions.
- Respect each other's needs and feelings.
- Have one meeting, with everyone present.
- Start and end on time. Return from breaks on time.
- Communicate openly and honestly. Avoid hidden agendas.
- Focus on issues. Avoid personal attacks.
- Look for the value in every idea.
- Participate fully.
- Work as a team, not a group of individuals.

Appendix B contains more information on creating and maintaining psychological safety in team meetings. As we examine the use of team processes and other ways to build the perfect team, we will discuss additional ground rules to further enhance team performance.

## Conclusion

Team norms are the glue that binds a team together. Each team must set its own norms, which may include the ones previously mentioned or others they feel will best support them in their collective work. Team norms work best when they are organic. Set, use, add, delete, or revise them as necessary to provide the maximum support to the team as it evolves to face new challenges.

# Chapter 3

## Transition from Group to Team

The third step in building the perfect team is to guide the team through the essential transition from a collection of individuals to a high-performing team. This transition has three stages—*dependence, counterdependence,* and *interdependence.*[8] Most groups get stuck in the *dependence* stage and never achieve their full potential. Here is a brief overview of the process of evolution from a group to a team.

All groups that meet on an ongoing basis go through the same three stages:

- *Dependence:* The leader convenes the group. The group depends on the leader to provide structure and keep them on track.
- *Counterdependence:* This is the painful adolescent stage, a transitional stage all groups go through. Adolescence is a time of stress and strain. The growing child tests the limits of parental control. The parents struggle to maintain authority while allowing limited independence. The ultimate goal is for the adolescent to learn to make mature, independent decisions. As the group matures, the members develop a desire to take over more of the responsibilities of leadership. There is give and take as the leader tests their readiness and gradually shares responsibility.
- *Interdependence:* This occurs when the leader and the group learn to share leadership responsibility. This is a high-performing stage in which the group, now a smoothly functioning team, performs at peak effectiveness.

The greatest challenges to the team leader occur in the second (counterdependence) stage. This is a normal stage of group development, even in groups made up of cooperative people. At first, a group depends on its leader, which generally results in a low level of conflict and reasonable performance. However, the group must assume responsibility for its own process at some point to develop into a high-performing, self-directed team.[9] At this point, the potential for conflict is highest and the demands on the leader's conflict management skills and commitment to building the perfect team by achieving interdependence is the greatest.

In the counterdependence stage, outspoken group members typically confront the leader. The stronger, more controlling ones often ask questions or make comments like:

- "Why are we doing this? It is not getting us anywhere."
- "Why don't we do things the way we did before?"
- "I know a better way to do this."

Sometimes these people have the group's best interest, as well as their own, at heart when they voice their feelings; at other times, their motives are purely selfish. When group members raise objections, it is your responsibility as leader to help the group work through the issues.

To manage challenges to your leadership when they occur in the counterdependence stage, use this five-step process:

1. Remind the group they must work through this stage in order to reach their goal of shared leadership.
2. Insist they decide by consensus on any changes in direction or approach.

3. Ask any person who challenges your leadership or the group's progress to suggest an alternative.
4. Ask the group to decide on the merits of the suggested alternative.
5. Change the group's agenda or process to reflect the new focus if the group agrees with the alternative. If they do not agree, help the team pick up where they were before the challenger objected.

As the leader, you must hold on to the reins until the group dynamics indicate that the members are ready (mature enough as a team) to share leadership responsibility. At that point (the interdependence stage) you turn leadership over to the team. Appendix C contains more information about how to manage conflicts that occur between team members in meetings.

# Chapter 4

## Adopt the Team Leadership Model

As you facilitate the transition of the team to the shared leadership (interdependence) stage of team development, you use a team leadership model to focus the team on the right issues in the right way.

The most important decision a team leader has to make is the choice of a leadership style.[10] The choices range from being autocratic (using top-down decision-making processes) to being participative (using collaborative decision-making processes). The choice depends on the leader's view of how best to motivate team members to get the job done—by encouraging an individual-oriented, competitive group dynamic or a team-oriented, cooperative dynamic. An autocratic style engenders competition, while a participative style engenders collaboration. Which is the better choice?

Scientific evidence exists to help leaders make this crucial decision. An analysis of over 500 research studies showed that cooperative processes are generally superior to conflict-inducing, competitive processes in terms of team performance and member satisfaction.[11] As discussed previously, competition often prevents a group in stage one (dependence) from transitioning to high-performance team in stage three (interdependence). Hence, a leader is more likely to succeed in building the perfect team, all other things being equal, by adopting a participative leadership style. But what is the best way to implement a participative leadership style in a team setting?

James MacGregor Burns, Pulitzer Prize winning author, described the alternative to traditional, top-down leadership. He called it transforming leadership.[12] Burns argued that the essence of leadership is less about individualism and control than people development and the pursuit of a collective (common) purpose. Bradford and Cohen gave substance to the theory of transforming leadership. They argued that to lead an organization in the modern era, a leader must do three things:

1. Create a common vision of the future (a collective purpose).
2. Share responsibility for achieving that vision with followers.
3. Focus on developing the capability of individuals in the organization to perform at their best.[13]

This simple and elegant three-step process—Common Vision, Shared Responsibility, Developmental Focus—is the Modern Leadership Model (MLM).[14] The modern leadership model has its theoretical roots in the fundamentals of change management, particularly the paramount importance of collaborative processes to effective change. Consequently, its practical applications are remarkable for their ability to transform organizations.[15]

The Team Leadership Model (TLM), a version of the modern leadership model tailored to the needs of high-performing teams,[16] encourages leaders to:

1. *Develop a common vision of desired outcomes* from the team's efforts, both in general (for the achievement of their collective purpose) and for specific tasks they undertake in support of their collective purpose. [Common Vision]
2. *Share responsibility with team members for developing collaborative strategies and actions* to achieve the

desired outcomes. [Shared Responsibility]

3. *Develop team members' capabilities*, individually and collectively, to perform at their best to achieve the desired outcomes. [Development Focus]

Like applying the modern leadership model to organizations, the results of applying the team leadership model to teams can be quite dramatic, improving both the quality of the outcomes and the speed at which the team achieves them.

# Chapter 5

## Use Collaborative Problem-Solving Processes

Having (1) balanced your team; (2) set team norms to ensure psychological safety, engagement, and collaboration; (3) facilitated the transition from a group to a high-performing team; and (4) adopted the team leadership model, the next step in building the perfect team is (5) to use consensus-based, collaborative problem-solving and decision-making processes to identify, prioritize, and address the issues (problems and opportunities) that constitute the team's principal work.

Effective teams use a variety of collaborative problem-solving and decision-making processes, ranging from unstructured discussion regulated by collaborative norms to formal collaborative processes like the Nominal Group Technique (NGT).[17]

### Unstructured Discussion

The most familiar problem-solving and decision-making process is the traditional unstructured discussion. In this type of discussion, anyone who wishes to address an issue either raises their hand for recognition by the leader or, in smaller more informal groups, just speaks up. The burden is on the leader to figure out how to encourage full participation and keep the team on track. One good way to do that is to create and encourage the use of team norms that engage everyone in the discussion in a psychologically safe way, like those discussed in Chapter 2.

## Brainstorming

Brainstorming is a somewhat structured approach for generating a large number of ideas quickly. After establishing some basic rules, the leader solicits ideas, which team members contribute at random and without evaluation. The team members build (piggyback) on each other's ideas to improve them and generate more ideas. In a separate process conducted after the initial brainstorming session, the team evaluates the ideas, identifying and focusing on those with high merit and ignoring those of lesser value. For more on collaborative brainstorming, including how to set norms for and conduct a productive brainstorming session, see Appendix D.

Note that the separation of the process into two stages, idea generation followed by constructive evaluation of the ideas, makes brainstorming work best. When the leader does not keep the two steps separate, participants often feel free to criticize other team members' ideas when and if they feel like it. Brainstorming of this kind seldom works, as negative criticism undermines the norms of psychological safety. Lack of psychological safety is why so many group problem-solving efforts fail.

## Force Field Analysis

Force Field Analysis is a technique for identifying the forces that work in favor of or against the team's achieving a goal or course of action. Team members brainstorm a list of positive or supporting forces, and another list of negative or hindering forces. Next, they prioritize both lists based on the relative strength of the forces. Finally, they discuss ways to reduce the impact of the strongest negative forces. For more on Force Field Analysis, see Appendix E.

## Collaborative Decision-Making Model

Decision-making methods take many forms, from applying basic models involving a series of predefined steps to the application of complex, mathematical decision models. The basic decision-making model consists of 7 steps designed to lead the team to a conclusion about the best alternative to choose to solve a problem or capitalize on an opportunity:

| Decision-Making Model | |
|---|---|
| **Step** | **Purpose** |
| 1. Problem | 1. Identify the real problem. |
| 2. Objective | 2. Determine the overall objective. |
| 3. Alternatives | 3. Identify the alternatives. |
| 4. Analysis | 4. Analyze the alternatives. |
| 5. Decision | 5. Decide on the best solution. |
| 6. Implementation | 6. Implement the decision. |
| 7. Assessment | 7. Assess the decision's impact. |

When applying the model, you first identify the real problem. For example, is the problem that a group of employees need training in effective customer service or is the real problem that they have a bad manager whose mistreatment of them results in poor customer service. Then, you determine the objective. How will you know if you have solved the problem? When costs are X% lower, measured performance is Y% higher, customer service scores have improved by Z%, or the chosen alternative meets or exceeds the required improvement in some other set of key performance indicators? Knowing what the real problem is and how you will know when you have solved it sets the stage for identifying the alternatives, analyzing them, and deciding which one will best solve the problem. Having decided on the best solution to the problem, you must then figure out how to implement the chosen alternative, which you will learn about in the next chapter, and then assess whether the intended solution worked and, if not, what to do next.

Caveat: When applying this classic decision-making process, it is essential to follow the norms you have agreed upon to guide the team, and if necessary to create new norms to ensure that the team works collaboratively and effectively to solve the identified problem.

There are many possible ways to complete each of the 7 steps in the Classic Decision-Making Model successfully. In Appendix F, we examine how to apply each of the 7 steps of the decision-making model from a classic and a collaborative perspective to illustrate differences in the two approaches.

## Ideal State Analysis

Ideal State Analysis (ISA) is a method for setting and achieving transformative goals.[18] In the traditional problem-solving approach, the team generates a list of alternatives for improving the current state (C) and chooses the best one, subject to whatever constraints or limitations they have imposed on the solution. This approach, while technically correct, often results in narrow (inside-the-box) thinking that produces a future state (B) which is a better but often just an incremental improvement over the current state.

When applying ideal state analysis, the team imagines what an ideal future state (A) would look like. The ideal future state represents a significant improvement in performance over the current state (C) and the traditional future state (B). That is, A is much better than B or C. They then decide what steps are necessary to reach that ideal future state. This process encourages breakthrough thinking. Because team members often find they have similar visions of the ideal future state, and because achieving it presents an exciting challenge, ideal state analysis energizes the team to think creatively about ways to bridge the gap between A and C.

Ideal State Analysis is a very powerful tool. I recommend that you explain it to the team before they start working together to solve problems, so they can use it to maximize their effectiveness from the outset. For more on Ideal State Analysis, see Appendix G.

## Nominal Group Technique

Like brainstorming, the Nominal Group Technique (NGT) is a combination of a brainstorming method and an evaluation method. However, it is much more sophisticated, consensus-based approach. NGT has a wide range of uses in team meetings, from creating (by consensus) an agenda for a specific meeting to identifying and prioritizing (by consensus) the key problems and opportunities the team faces. While the 10-step nominal group technique process looks complicated, it is simple to apply and typically has a transformative effect on a team's ability to work together to solve problems. Appendix H contains an example of how to apply the Nominal Group Technique to arrive at a team decision based on consensus.

# Chapter 6

## Apply Participative Implementation Processes

The point of having a great team is to make excellent decisions and implement them successfully. While there are many ways to try to do this, the most effective is to apply a proven implementation model in a participative manner. Such a model is Lewin's three-stage change model— Unfreezing, Moving, and Refreezing—also known as the UMR model.[19]

Caveat: Do not let the apparent simplicity of Lewin's model fool you. As his biographer said, "Freud the clinician and Lewin the experimentalist . . . are the two men whose names will stand out before all others in the history of our psychological era."[20] To paraphrase Mark Twain, the difference between Lewin's UMR model (an elegant and practical guide to dealing with the complex issues inherent in the change process[21]) and other change models is like the difference between lightning and the lightning bug. Let's see why.

### Lewin's UMR Model

Organizational change is the flip side of the leadership coin. The epitome of the modern leader is the transformational (i.e., transforming) leader. Traditional leaders focus on doing things right, while transformational leaders focus on doing the right thing.[22]

In terms of leadership and organizational change, the first step in the Lewin process involves unfreezing the current situation (the current state) to overcome inherent resistance to change. Leaders can do this in one of two ways. Old style, command-and-control leaders either point to an existing, survival-threatening crisis that demands immedi-ate action or, in cases where there is no real crisis, manufac-ture one to compel their subordinates to act. While this sometimes succeeds in motivating organization members to take appropriate action in the short term, more often than not it also increases long-term resistance to change from the people in the organization who feel that their leaders have manipulated and taken advantage of them.

A second, much more effective way to unfreeze the situa-tion is to engage affected employees and other stakeholders in the process of creating a vision of the future and encour-age and empower them to work together to make it a reali-ty. President John F. Kennedy did that when he announced on national television that America would put a man on the moon by the end of the sixties and empowered NASA to make it happen. This second method of unfreezing a situa-tion is the only choice for a transformational leader when the organization does not face a crisis. In those instances when there is a legitimate crisis, a transformational leader could unfreeze the current state by explaining to the people in the organization how the crisis arose and asking them to work together with management to resolve the situation. To reiterate, when applying the first step of the Lewin change model (unfreezing) a leader who wants to effect meaningful change must not make the mistake of exaggerating an existing crisis or faking one when none exists. While this type of overt manipulation is a standard practice for com-mand-and-control leaders, it has no place in the repertoire of the transformational leader.

When the leader has unfrozen the situation, the actual change can occur. The change or movement of the system can result from an intervention aimed at the individual, team, or organizational level. Training employees to use a new system is an example of an individual-level intervention. Team building to empower a newly redesigned work group is an example of a team-level intervention. Process reengineering and organizational restructuring are examples of interventions aimed at organization-wide change. In this second (moving) step, the leader once again has important decisions to make that can derail, delay, or accelerate the change process. The interventions chosen to facilitate the change (movement) can succeed or fail depending on how the leader introduces and manages them.

Traditional leaders decide unilaterally what is good for the individual, group, or organization. For example, command-and-control leaders often mandate training for specific individuals as the solution to problems that are really the result of systemic forces, such as inadequate organizational structure, ineffective reward systems, and bad management, and which are, therefore, beyond the control of any individual. Similarly, top-down leaders often view team building as the solution to problems that really stem from poor meeting management or inept leadership. And hierarchical leaders often initiate organization level change efforts, such as reengineering and total quality management, because key competitors adopt them or outside consultants suggest them as best practices, regardless of whether they make sense for the organization.

Transformational leaders avoid these top-down interventions, except in those rare cases when unilateral action is necessary to avert a crisis. Instead, they take the time to engage the members of the organization in a change effort based on shared vision, joint problem identification, collaborative problem solving, mutual support throughout the change process, and joint evaluation and re-visioning.

When it comes to refreezing (institutionalizing) the changes, once again the difference between transformational leaders and old-style leaders is significant. Top-down leaders order the organization members affected by the change to follow the new procedures, systems, or policies. Transformational leaders, having secured buy-in at each stage of the change process, support those organization members in manifesting the attitudes and taking the actions necessary to ensure the permanence of the new system.

For example, if misguided leaders simply tell their people that they are empowering them to act, without taking the time to develop their trust or indicate what they mean by empowered action, people will not take the initiative to adopt new, more risk-taking behaviors, or worse will take the wrong actions. Conversely, if leaders effect change by means of participative processes designed to encourage and support innovation and creativity, they stimulate a number of high-quality suggestions from people who are willing to share the responsibility for implementing them.

As argued in the preceding paragraphs, leaders can use Lewin's three-stage (UMR) model either effectively or ineffectively. Typically, top-down leaders violate its implicit assumptions at each stage and do not get the results they want; whereas more collaborative, transformational leaders intuitively understand its participative nature and use it to effect meaningful change.[23]

In my experience as a leader and facilitator of planned, systemic change, the best way to initiate, facilitate, and ensure project success is to (1) unfreeze by engaging stakeholders early and actively in a collaborative dialogue about the change effort; (2) initiate and sustain movement by continuing the high level of two-way communication, joint action planning, and shared implementation effort; and (3) refreeze to a higher level of individual and organizational performance and satisfaction by reinforcing the commitment to project success based on continued collaboration for the duration of the project and beyond.[24] You will find an example of how to apply the UMR model in Appendix I.

# Chapter 7

## Facilitate Team and Organizational Learning

The final step in building the perfect team involves regular assessment of team processes and outcomes with a view to continued team development and organizational improvement. Lewin described this process as Action Research.[25] Senge referred to it as Organizational Learning.[26] Lewin suggested that after you have acted, you must do some research to determine what worked and what did not, and why, and take whatever new actions are necessary to achieve the desired outcomes. Senge argued that after you have acted, you must learn from what happened and share what you learn with others in the organization to improve overall system performance.

Whether you track team performance informally by means of ad hoc reviews, or formally by means of scheduled team performance reviews, it is imperative that you monitor task work and teamwork, both of which are critical to team performance. The team, not outsiders, must conduct their own performance reviews using the consensus-building, collaborative processes described in Chapter 5 to rate their task work and teamwork, identify the underlying problems, and resolve them. A high level of task work and teamwork is what you should expect from the perfect team. If the team exhibits one characteristic, but not the other, you do not have a perfect team. You have a problem that needs fixing.

The table depicts an array of the possible combinations of task work and teamwork, from high performance (A, high task work and high teamwork) to low performance (F, low task work and low teamwork).

| TASK WORK | High | C | B | A |
|-----------|--------|---|---|---|
|           | Medium | E | D | B |
|           | Low | F | E | C |
|           |      | Low | Medium | High |
|           |      | TEAMWORK | | |

If the consensus is that team performance is at level A, you have a high-performance team. If performance is at level B because task work is high but teamwork is only at a medium level, the team needs to take action to improve their teamwork, such as reviewing the identified problems and setting new team norms to prevent them from recurring. Conversely, if performance is at level B because teamwork is high but task work is only at a medium level, the team needs to take action to improve their task work, such as determining how to improve their project development process if that is the identified problem. If team performance is at level D, actions to improve both task work and teamwork are necessary to reach level A (high performance). Level E and F performance will necessitate even more drastic team actions to achieve Level A performance.

This final step in building the perfect team brings the team full circle. Action based on the research conducted in this final step of the process leads to new actions to achieve and/or maintain high team performance, followed by assessment (research) to determine the results of those actions and identify new actions needed to maintain or enhance team effectiveness. This continuous cycle of team improvement in which the team takes responsibility for managing its own learning is the hallmark of an *interdependent* team.

# Chapter 8

## Summary of the Perfect Team Model

To build the perfect team, you must:

1. *Balance the Team* by including individuals with hard and soft skills, different ways of thinking, diversity and cultural awareness, and user perspective.
2. *Create* norms that foster *Psychological Safety*, engagement, and collaboration.
3. *Transition from Group to Team* by leading the team through the three stages of development from dependence to counterdependence to interdependence (high performance).
4. *Adopt the Team Leadership Model* to focus the team on the right issues in the right way.
5. *Use Collaborative Problem-Solving Processes* to identify, prioritize, and address the problems (or opportunities) that constitute the team's principal work.
6. *Apply Participative Implementation Processes* to ensure change that resolves the problems (or capitalizes on the opportunities).
7. *Facilitate Team and Organizational Learning* through regular assessment of team processes and outcomes with a view to continued team development and organizational improvement.

# Appendices

# Appendix A

## Using MBTI to Balance the Team

As described in Chapter 1, to build the perfect team you must make sure the team has good balance. This means having people with relevant hard and soft skills who think differently, are diverse and culturally aware, and understand the needs and capabilities of the people affected by the team's work. Having people who think differently helps to avoid group think and other dysfunctional group problems, such as the inability (a) to engage all team members in the group process, (b) collect the hard and soft data needed to truly understand issues, (c) make decisions that balance logic with values, and (d) strike a balance between task work and teamwork.

Achieving team balance is an art, not a science. Fortunately, the findings of research about the application of the Myers-Briggs Type Indicator (MBTI), a well-known scientific approach to measuring individuals' preference in each of four dimensions [Extroversion—Introversion (E/I), Sensing—iNtuition (S/N), Thinking—Feeling (T/F), and Judging—Perceiving (J/P)], provides insights into how to avoid these common group problems.

### Engaging All Team Members

Many groups underachieve because a few highly vocal individuals dominate the group process. In a typical group, MBTI experts estimate that there are three extroverts for each introvert.[28] Add to this the fact that extroverts prefer to talk before they think, while introverts prefer to think before they talk, and you have a prescription for lack of engagement of the introverts on the team. One way to reduce the effect is to ensure that the number of introverts is closer to 50% than 25%. Another way is to create team norms for ensuring engagement, psychological security, and collaboration, like those suggested in Chapter 2:

- Give everyone a chance to speak during team discussions.
- Respect each other's needs and feelings.
- Have one meeting, with everyone present.
- Start and end on time. Return from breaks on time.
- Communicate openly and honestly. Avoid hidden agendas.
- Focus on issues. Avoid personal attacks.
- Look for the value in every idea.
- Participate fully.
- Work as a team, not a group of individuals.

## Collecting and Analyzing Data for Decision Making

There are two types of data, hard and soft. Both are necessary to make good decisions. Hard data are measurable facts. Soft data are intangibles, such as opinions, perceptions, feelings, and values. Basing decisions on the facts may sound like the only way to go. However, consider the possibility of making a valid but really bad decision due to not including essential factors that are not readily quantifiable. For example, the numbers might suggest that the right decision is to close a historically profitable manufacturing plant because of the disruptive impact of other companies moving their plants to countries where labor is cheaper and other inducements are available. A better decision might be to engage plant employees in a collaborative effort to find a way out of the situation involving joint initiatives that lead to greater profits through reductions in overhead and improvements in worker productivity. In the first case, managers ignore the intangibles and make the decision that radical change is necessary without considering the effect on employees and without involving them in the decision-making process. In the second case, managers choose to deal with intangible factors such as the loyalty and productivity demonstrated historically by their employees, the likelihood that a joint solution might be even better in the long run, and the willingness of their employees to actively implement a joint decision to ensure that the required changes take place in a timely manner.

Sensing types rely on concrete data when making decisions; intuitive types grasp the big picture without the need for much sensory data. Thinkers prefer to decide based on logic; feeling types make decisions based on their potential impact on people. Thus, sensing, thinking people rely primarily on logical analysis of hard data to make decisions, while intuitive, feeling people rely primarily on intuitive analysis of soft data to make decisions. To achieve balance, you need both types of decision makers on the team. If you think of logical analysis of hard data as left brain thinking and intuitive insight based on soft data as right brain thinking, a team must have a whole brain approach to collecting data and making decisions, whether each person makes decisions this way or the team as a whole makes decisions this way.

## Balancing Task Work and Teamwork

Judging types are planners who seek closure; perceiving types are more spontaneous and prefer to leave their options open. One important way in which this manifests itself is the focus of judging types on task work, at times at the expense of teamwork, and the opposite focus of perceiving types on teamwork, at times at the expense of task work. A perfect team must find the right balance of task work and teamwork necessary to operate at peak productivity. Having a mix of judging and perceiving types on the team helps make this possible.

# Appendix B

## Creating Psychological Safety

Team norms are the glue that binds a team together; particularly, those that create psychological safety. The challenge for all organizations that use teams is to figure out how to instill these essential group norms in their teams. One way would be to make these norms mandatory team behaviors. This has a certain appeal, especially if you believe that the presence of the norms is sufficient to result in heightened team performance. In practice, however, this approach has several problems. First, many teams include people who are uncomfortable sharing their feelings or do not care about the feelings of others to the degree required to ensure the psychological safety of their teammates. Second, taking a rule-based approach to institutionalizing behavior can create problems, instead of solving them. For example, telling an introvert that they must speak because it is their turn is more likely to induce anxiety in the introvert than to create a sense of psychological safety. So, what can an organization determined to improve the success rate of its teams do to encourage team members to exhibit the two essential behaviors of Google's most successful teams—listening to each other and being sensitive to feelings and needs?

Given the pervasiveness of teams in organizations and the chronically high average project failure rates, a two-stage approach to instilling these two essential behaviors seems justified. First, do something to create quick wins in the short term. Then engage in a more ambitious effort that addresses the root causes of the problem to develop sustainable changes in behavior.

In the short term, a more effective alternative than mandating that teams adopt practices based on norms of conversational turn taking and heightened social sensitivity is to do what a good group facilitator would do—suggest that existing teams experiment with a collaborative process for establishing team ground rules, which starts by encouraging people to listen to each other. Team members should discuss the importance to their success as a team of hearing from everyone on the team who has something to say on an issue. They should ensure that all team members who wish to speak have a chance to speak, but only when they are ready, not when it is "their turn." They should create a ground rule to ensure that this happens consistently and write down and display it, along with the other team ground rules, at all team meetings. If the team lapses into old habits, it should self-correct by returning to the established practice of giving everyone a chance to speak. Repeated over time, this behavior will become a standard practice, which is the operational definition of a group norm. To encourage people to be sensitive to their team members' feelings and needs, the team should develop a ground rule for it using this collaborative process for establishing team ground rules.

The work of Kurt Lewin, a pioneer in the field of group dynamics, provides theoretical support for Google's empirical findings and the experiential knowledge of group facilitators about group norms. Lewin argued that behavior is the result of interaction between a person ($P$) and the environment ($E$): Behavior $= f(P, E)$.[27] If the goal is to improve the odds of project success by requiring teams to adopt group norms to create psychological safety, such as the two norms identified by Google as being characteristic of its most successful teams, then Lewin's formula suggests that a way to make this happen would be to create an environment ($E$) that supports the use of such norms, and select individuals for important team projects with a predisposition, based on their personality $(P)$, to want to listen to others and work with them to solve problems.

If teams were not so pervasive, this might be all that would be necessary to achieve the goal. However, many potential team members with skills or knowledge required for team success may not be team players; therefore, the real problem is to determine how to change the behaviors of these individuals when they are working on team projects to ensure that they work effectively with the other team members. One approach, as we have seen, is to mandate that all team members adhere to the two group norms. However, telling people what to do is seldom a good idea. Another approach is to require all team members to attend some form of group-process training; however, this could be time consuming and the skills learned might not be transferable to the real team setting. Fortunately, modern change management principles, based on the work of Lewin, provide the additional insights needed to solve this challenging problem.

Mandating the use of the two essential norms for team success is one way to encourage their use, as Google discovered in the process of conducting research into the perfect team. This is essentially a top-down solution. An alternative, using change management principles provides a collaborative alternative that is arguably much better. One change model, which many organizational change experts use, is Lewin's three-stage model. The three steps in Lewin's model are unfreezing, moving, and refreezing (UMR). Underlying Lewin's model is the basic field-theory formulation captured in the equation: Behavior $= f(P, E)$.

How might we motivate team members, particularly those who are not team players by nature, to adopt those two

ground rules for creating psychological safety?[28] Lewin
suggested that the best way to unfreeze a situation was to
reduce the strength of the forces that were hindering movement in the desired direction. In this case, these forces
would include (a) a lack of incentive to change, (b) teams
with a history of not having operated based on norms, and
(c) people's natural resistance to change. Notice that the top-
down strategy, insisting on mandatory use, would probably
result in a strengthening of the hindering forces due to people's natural resistance to change.

A change management approach to *unfreezing* (U) the
situation, based on Lewin's model, would require management to communicate the need for change, with the goal of
sharing and discussing the findings of the Google perfect-
team research, and engaging all employees in a common
goal of improving project success by working more collaboratively. This approach would include adopting the norms that
produce psychological safety as ground rules for team behavior. Note the subtle, but important, difference between the
mandatory-use strategy (a push strategy) and the engagement strategy (a pull strategy). The former tends to create
resentment in employees, while the latter tends to empower
them.

In the *moving* phase (M) of the change management approach, teams would try out the new ground rules and share
their experiences with the new norms and others that
emerged as helpful to team success, in an organized, collaborative effort aimed at team and organizational learning and
development. Finally, in the *refreezing* phase (R), teams
would voluntarily commit to ongoing use of the new set of
ground rules and team norms, because these rules and
norms work for them, not because they are mandatory.
Arguably, the engagement-oriented, collaborative change

management process would be much more likely to achieve the desired goal of universal use of the psychological safety ground rules by all teams.

# Appendix C

## Managing Team Conflicts

All meetings have conflicts.[29] They can be as minor as a disagreement between someone who dominates the conversation and someone else who does not appreciate it, or as serious as a clenched-fist shouting match. Traditional meeting leaders think that conflict is bad. They try to ignore it or brush it aside. This is a mistake. A conflict-free meeting is neither possible nor desirable.

Conflict is a warning sign of underlying problems. When it arises, the leader needs to bring it under control. Otherwise the problems will fester and interfere with the team's work. Conflict provides an opportunity to identify and remove obstacles before they impede progress.

The three major sources of meeting conflict, listed from most common to least common, are:

- The natural evolution from group to team
- Differences in people's personality
- Disruptive people

### The Group's Evolution

We discussed the three stages that all groups go through as they mature into teams (dependence, counterdependence, and interdependence) and how to manage the conflicts that occur in the challenging counterdependence stage in Chapter 3.

## Differing Personality Types

Psychologists classify people into personality types based on the ways they think and behave. When people with contrasting personality types work together, they sometimes clash because of their dissimilar ways of perceiving and acting. The leader's job is to monitor this tension to ensure that friction does not develop into full-blown conflict.

The two most common personality-related clashes are:

- Extroverts versus introverts
- Quick versus deliberate decision makers

### *Extroverts versus Introverts*

Extroverts like to express themselves. They are outspoken and often speak without thinking. Introverts are the opposite. They prefer to organize their thoughts before talking. Introverts are quiet and sometimes appear unexpressive. But when they speak, they typically add value to the meeting. Misunderstandings between extroverts and introverts are common. Extroverts complain that introverts don't speak up at the right time in meetings. Introverts criticize extroverts for talking too much and not listening well. The extroverts, if allowed to, will dominate the discussion. The introverts end up annoyed because the extroverts use up all the time allotted for discussion. Unless the leader resolves the conflict, introverts may react by not participating fully or by using indirect methods to hinder the team's progress.

Bearing in mind that the contributions of both extroverts and introverts are important to a high-performance team, manage conflicts between these two personality types by taking the following steps:

- Ask each side to state clearly what it wants from the other.
- Help the team to develop ground rules to relieve the sources of conflict identified in the first step.
- Help the team to enforce the rules when necessary.

### Quick versus Deliberate Decision Makers

Two other types that often butt heads during a team meeting are those who like to decide quickly and those who prefer to make up their minds only after exploring all their options. Extroverts can be either quick or deliberate decision makers; the same goes for introverts. Clashes between quick and deliberate types often surface early in the life of a team, during the time spent on process and initial team development. Quick decision makers tend to focus on the work and to complain about time spent on process. Deliberate decision makers tend to see process as highly important. Conflict surfaces again during the later stages of a meeting when the team is working on its tasks. If the team doesn't spend enough time maintaining team processes and managing teamwork, the deliberate decision makers are likely to object.

Here are some tips on resolving these conflicts:

- Point out that a proper balance between process (teamwork) and content (task work) is essential to team effectiveness. New teams, while they are learning new processes or ways of operating, need to spend more time on process than experienced teams. Expe-

rienced teams, regardless of how well they are working together, need to spend time maintaining the effi-
ciency of their processes.
- Encourage each side to say what it wants and help
  the team to develop appropriate ground rules.
- Help the team to enforce the rules when necessary.

Sometimes you can help through your actions. For example, if the deliberate decision makers are becoming
uncomfortable because things are moving too fast, you can
slow the process down by reviewing the discussion and
summarizing the agreements reached. You can also help by
talking to one side or the other before the meeting or during
a break. Use this time to assess their level of frustration and
to reassure them if they need it.

If you have quick and deliberate decision makers on your
team, which you probably do, you have to help them manage
the tension that results. It never goes away completely. The
best you can hope for is that in the end both will feel that
they got most of what they wanted out of the meeting and
that the improvement in team performance far outweighed
any compromises they had to make.

## Managing Disruptive People

Disruptive people are uncooperative because they believe it
is in their best interest for the team to fail. Here are four of
the most frequently encountered categories of disruptive
people:

### Misguided Team Members

Some team members fear that they will lose power if group dynamics change as a result of adopting a more collaborative approach to problem solving and decision making.

### Outsiders with Vested Interests

These are people from other divisions or organizations who have a vested interest in a particular policy or position . Such representatives often have instructions to support their organization's interests and sabotage any threat to those interests.

### Natural Competitors

Natural competitors feel uncomfortable in a cooperative atmosphere. These people derive their personal satisfaction from bumping heads with others. Instead of cooperating, they look for ways to upset every meeting they attend, particularly those in which the participants strive for active participation and teamwork.

### People Who Bear a Grudge Against the Company

These are people upset or frustrated over such issues as company policy or the way their manager treats them.

Fortunately, you don't run into truly disruptive people very often. When you do, however, you must take decisive action. The question is: "How do you know when you're dealing with a disruptive person?" Most disruptive people reveal themselves in the initial stage of team formation.

However, not everyone who asks probing questions at that time is a problem person. Because all change is threatening, it is natural for people to feel uncomfortable with a new team or approach and ask questions or raise objections in the beginning. If you respond with patience and tact to their concerns, most participants agree to suspend judgment and permit the team to continue. Disruptive people do not. Instead, realizing that the situation is most tenuous at the beginning, they attack. Their goal is to keep the group from forming into a team by discrediting you, the leader, or by polarizing the team.

If the disruptive individual persists and you suspect you are dealing with a problem person, make sure that the conflict doesn't fit either of the patterns described earlier in this appendix, counterdependent behavior or a personality clash, before you act. Conflicts resulting from group evolution or differing personality types are predictable and manageable. The infrequent conflicts caused by disruptive individuals are harder to manage. Here is a four-step method for dealing with these situations:

### *Deflect Any Personal Attacks*

Probe to discover the issue or problem behind the personal criticism. Try to determine whether the person's question or objection is legitimate or intentionally disruptive.

### *Go Public*

Don't try to handle the disruptive person by yourself. Get the team to do it. Ask the team members whether they agree with the criticism. If they don't agree, you may have a disruptive person on your hands. If they agree, the individual may have a legitimate concern. Ask the team whether this has happened before and what impact it has had on their ability to work as a team. Ask what they intend to do about it.

### *Urge the Team to Create Ground Rules to Deal with the Disruptive Behavior*

If the team does this and the same individual continues to violate the rules, ask them to consider punishment, such as expulsion from the team.

### *Take a Break*

If step three doesn't work, take a break. Try to reason with the disruptive individual. If this fails, adjourn the meeting. Meet with the disruptive person's manager and insist that they assign a more team-oriented person. Don't accept any excuses or promises to do better at this point. The success of the team is at stake. Be a leader; take a stand.

I hope that you as leader will never have to face a situation involving a disruptive individual. But if you do, and if the offender continues to be disruptive, summon your courage and do what you have to do for the good of the team. And do it quickly.

Over the years, I have dealt with thousands of people in meetings and I can think of only a handful who were genuinely disruptive people. Remember this the next time you try to handle a criticism or objection. The person may have a legitimate point. Don't jump to the conclusion that the person is wrong or misguided. Follow the processes described in this appendix to help you and the other team members decide how to manage the conflicts you face. They will work for you as they have for many others.

# Appendix D

## Collaborative Brainstorming

Earlier I mentioned four tools teams can use to improve the quality of their discussions—the Nominal Group Technique, Brainstorming, Force Field Analysis, and Ideal State Analysis. These same tools can help refocus the team if it gets off track.[30] For example, what if the team has worked on several tasks effectively but gets bogged down discussing the next one. What can you do to revitalize and refocus them on the task at hand? Try brainstorming.

### Idea Generation

Brainstorming is helpful when the team needs to generate lots of ideas quickly. It is also useful when the discussion bogs down. It refocuses the team's thinking and helps them regain their momentum.

In a storm, rain falls suddenly and intensely. In the first, idea generation stage of brainstorming, the team generates a storm of ideas. Here's how that works:

First, the leader states the four rules of brainstorming. If the team is not familiar with them, the recorder writes them on a board or flip chart. The rules are:

#### Go for Volume

Generate as many unedited ideas as possible in the time allotted.

### Defer Judgment

Adopt a "no criticism" ground rule. Inform participants that the evaluation phase will come later. This should restrain those who have the urge to criticize as soon as someone presents an idea they don't agree with. Be prepared to enforce the ground rule vigorously.

### Encourage Piggybacking

"Piggybacking" means building or expanding on other people's ideas. Remember, novel solutions are rare. Often, the ultimate answer is a combination of the best parts of several ideas.

### Capture Ideas in Summary Form

Have someone record each idea. Ask participants to permit the recorder to condense their ideas into a newspaper headline to avoid slowing the process down. If desired, audio record the session to prevent the details of good ideas from being lost.

Brainstorming works best if people feel uninhibited about presenting ideas, no matter how strange or unrealistic they may seem. Monitor the process to ensure that no one evaluates ideas as the team generates them. If someone says, "I don't think that's a good idea," stop the process and ask the offender to wait until the appropriate time (the evaluation phase) to comment on the quality of the ideas. If you let people get away with this behavior, they will kill the brainstorming.

I once worked with a group of engineers who were designing a new product on an extremely ambitious schedule; and they were behind. They were all bright and opinionated.

No comment went uncriticized, no criticism went unchallenged. Naturally, their group dynamics were atrocious. They fought at every opportunity.

I introduced them to the brainstorming technique, hoping to kill two birds with one stone. First, I thought brainstorming would help them to develop some creative new ideas. Second, I felt the brainstorming prohibition against making snap judgments would reduce the amount of conflict. As we tried it, I enforced the ground rules strictly, allowing no one to make any judgmental comments until the evaluation phase. We brainstormed ways for the group to get back on schedule. Slowly they began to realize that some of the other engineers actually had some pretty good ideas. This raised their level of mutual respect and trust and, in turn, increased their comfort level with each other. Within a surprisingly short period of time, the group was able to work together in a way that was never before possible. People who had disagreed vehemently during previous meetings started asking each other for advice on technical matters. In the end, the group was able to pull itself together in time to meet its product deadline.

Let's examine another problem that brainstorming can help a team to solve.

I once facilitated a meeting of a group of people who simply did not listen to each other. Whoever had the floor would start to make a comment and someone else would interject. The second person would start talking about a new topic without even acknowledging what the first person had said.

To remedy this situation, I had two choices. One was the direct approach. I could stop the discussion and counsel the group about the importance of active listening, have them create a ground rule requiring it, teach them how to do it, and then run them through some practice exercises. I concluded that this option would take too much time. The group needed a quick fix to get participants to start listening immediately.

The second alternative was to use brainstorming. As I was explaining the process, l emphasized the importance of piggybacking on ideas suggested by others. In order to piggyback, the participants had to listen carefully to the ideas as people generated them. This forced them to listen to one another. Once they started listening—really listening—they began to appreciate the quality of the ideas they were hearing. They quickly learned to piggyback on ideas and produce good solutions. Like the first group, this one was able to use brainstorming for dual purposes: to generate more and better ideas, and to improve their interpersonal interactions and teamwork.

## Evaluation

The second, evaluation phase of brainstorming, in which the group pinpoints ideas with the greatest promise, occurs only after the group finishes brainstorming. You can use any number of standard problem-solving and decision-making methods in evaluating the ideas from a brainstorming session. Here are three examples:

### Informal Process

Review the list of ideas. Discuss their relative merit. Stop when the team agrees it has selected the best idea.

## Quantitative Analysis

Agree on decision criteria and weights. List and discuss the pros and cons of each idea. Rate each idea from zero to ten (high) on each decision criterion. Multiply the rating on each criterion by the preassigned weight for that criterion. Add these numbers up for each idea. Compare the total scores of all the ideas. Identify the top three. Discuss the results as a group and agree on the best one.

## Nominal Group Technique

Use the steps of the Nominal Group Technique described in Appendix H to agree by consensus on the best ideas.

Note: By separating the idea generation phase of brainstorming from the evaluation phase, the leader ensures that the team focuses on creative thinking in the first phase and on precise evaluation in the second phase, not mixing up the two as frequently occurs in meetings. This two-step process results in a much better team product.

## Common Mistakes in Brainstorming

Three common errors in the use of brainstorming are:

## Failing to Act on the Ideas After Generating Them

Some people think that brainstorming is the end of the process. But a list of ideas, no matter how creative, will not solve your problem. You must do something with these ideas; namely, evaluate and act on them.

### Letting the Brainstorming Drag On

When the participants run out of energy or enthusiasm and start to slow down, it's time to stop brainstorming and start evaluating the ideas. Creative problem solving is an iterative process, not a linear one.

### Failing to Balance the Demands of Quick versus Deliberate Decision Makers

Those who like to make quick decisions will attempt to grab the first good idea and run with it. You have to keep them at bay until the team has generated all its ideas. The opposite problem occurs with people who enjoy exploring options but hate making decisions. Deliberate decision makers love brainstorming. They never want to stop generating ideas. Don't allow them to overextend the session. Seek a balance between the two that is acceptable to the team. Use the ground rules/collaborative team norms to help manage the session and arrive at the best solution.

# Appendix E

## Force Field Analysis

The term "force field" comes from physics. Force Field Analysis refers to the study of forces that simultaneously assist or resist the movement of an object. Use Force Field Analysis to identify the major forces that simultaneously help or hinder movement toward a desired goal.[31] By evaluating these forces, the team develops insight into ways of overcoming resistance and creating movement toward the desired result.

Let's look at an example: Top management is consolidating two corporate departments. Their goal is to provide uninterrupted customer service while making a smooth transition to the new organization.

Major forces working against a smooth transition include:

- The two departments have radically different cultures.
- The affected employees are worried about their jobs.

Major forces supporting the transition include:

- The people in both departments are senior professionals who perform well under pressure.
- They will work harder to keep their jobs.

By examining these two lists, the team might be able to determine techniques to increase the strength of forces in support of a smooth transition, or to reduce or neutralize those forces opposing it. It is usually more fruitful to look at the forces hindering the goal first. In this case, the team might suggest that management communicate their intentions about possible downsizing as honestly and quickly as possible, or that they hire outside experts to help them manage the transition effectively.

You can generate the lists of positive and negative forces used in a Force Field Analysis by using the brainstorming technique. After completing the two lists, take the process one step further by placing them in order of priority. Start with the negative list and concentrate on the most important forces first.

Define the desired goal as specifically as possible. If you define the end result too loosely, your lists of positive or negative forces may be off the mark. Remember to prioritize each list, especially if you end up with many forces, and to concentrate on the most crucial three to five forces. Sometimes when doing a Force Field Analysis, the team will identify an opposing force that appears to be insurmountable. Encourage the team to keep hunting for solutions, assuming that the problem is not as big as it appears to be. If a team starts to believe that there is no solution, this view becomes a self-fulfilling prophecy. The leader's role is to maintain an atmosphere that is positive and action oriented. Assume that there is a solution for every problem. Make things happen. Don't allow the team to get bogged down in negative thoughts.

When used properly, Force Field Analysis is a powerful tool that a team can use to analyze and solve problems or sharpen the focus of a faltering team discussion.

# Appendix F

## Collaborative Decision Making

To understand how to conduct a collaborative decision-making process using the basic decision-making model, we will examine the application of each of the 7 steps listed in the table below (for the hypothetical example of resistance to change) from a classic and collaborative perspective to illustrate differences in the two approaches.

| Decision-Making Model | |
|---|---|
| **Step** | **Purpose** |
| 1. Problem | 1. Identify the real problem. |
| 2. Objective | 2. Determine the overall objective. |
| 3. Alternatives | 3. Identify the alternatives. |
| 4. Analysis | 4. Analyze the alternatives. |
| 5. Decision | 5. Decide on the best solution. |
| 6. Implementation | 6. Implement the decision. |
| 7. Assessment | 7. Assess the decision's impact. |

## 1. Problem

*Classic*: Accept the problem specified by management—workers resist change due to their inability to deal with the rate of change—as the real problem.

*Collaborative*: Accept this problem specification from management as the presenting problem but engage affected workers in a process of determining why they resist change to determine the real problem—workers are not part of the decision-making process, so they have neither the understanding of the need for change nor the time to implement the changes properly.

## 2. Objective

*Classic*: The overall objective is to implement change efficiently.

*Collaborative*: The overall objective is to engage employees effectively in the change process to ensure successful implementation and ongoing use of the new methods, while increasing employee job satisfaction.

## 3. Alternatives

*Classic*: Identify possible alternative solutions to the problem.

*Collaborative*: Involve key stakeholders, workers in this case, in the process of generating possible solutions with the team. Use collaborative decision-making processes and practices, such as those discussed in Chapter 5, to facilitate the work of the extended team.

## 4. Analysis

*Classic*: Use hard data and quantitative analytical tools, such as decision matrix analysis, or a more elaborate decision model developed using Management Science methods, to estimate the effects of each alternative.

*Collaborative*: Apply a collaborative problem-solving process, such as those described in Chapter 5, to do a comparative analysis of the alternatives using both quantitative methods (such as decision matrix analysis) and qualitative methods (such as pros and cons analysis) to determine the effects of each alternative.

## 5. Decision

*Classic*: Decide on the best alternative based exclusively on the outcome of the Analysis step.

*Collaborative*: Based on the outcome of the Analysis step, engage the extended team in a whole-brain (using left-brain logic and right brain intuition) discussion of the qualitative (not measurable) as well as quantitative (measurable) aspects of the alternatives to determine the best solution.

## 6. Implementation

*Classic*: Communicate and implement the best solution in a top-down fashion.

*Collaborative*: Use a participative implementation process (see Chapter 6) such as Lewin's three-stage UMR change model to engage users affected by the change in the process to get buy-in, reduce resistance to change, and increase the chance of a successful implementation of the best solution.

## 7. Assessment

*Classic*: Determine if the change worked and why for management control purposes.

*Collaborative*: Facilitate team development and organizational learning by conducting a planned review of the outcomes of the change process, as described in Chapter 7.

# Appendix G

## Ideal State Analysis

Managers often hold meetings to plan for the future. The team has to decide how an organization can move from where it is now to where it wants to be in the future. To set the stage for an examination of Ideal State Analysis (ISA)[32], let's look at a company that currently markets its products only in the United States but wants to market throughout Europe within 3 years. The president calls a kickoff meeting of his team (key managers and staff) to produce a plan for achieving that goal.

Because the traditional planning approach emphasizes starting with existing conditions, the team examines the various problems and constraints involved in marketing their product in the United States. They then base the European plan on their U.S. experience. As this product has achieved the second highest market share of the major competitors in the United States after much time and great expense, they decide that an ambitious but realistic goal would be to achieve the same market-share ranking in Europe in 3 years.

The problem with this traditional approach is that the team becomes so grounded in the current state that they are often blind to other possible outcomes. They never ask themselves what they really want. If the ideal state would be to achieve a number-one market share within 2 years, why not use Ideal State Analysis, a very powerful tool for enabling teams to achieve their full potential, to figure out how to become #1?

Here is how to do use Ideal State Analysis in a meeting:

1. Start by asking the team to briefly describe the present situation (the Current State). Record the highlights of the discussion. Put them aside for later use.
2. Establish the ground rule that everyone is to use possibility thinking during the Ideal State Analysis; that is, participants are to assume that anything is possible (that there are no constraints).
3. Ask each participant to answer the question: What is the Ideal State? They are to describe what the ideal future would be like if it were exactly the way they wanted it.
4. Have each person summarize their Ideal State individually.
5. Display and compare these individual Ideal States, searching for common areas among the ideas.
6. Arrive at a consensus of the Ideal State. This becomes the goal.
7. Have the team brainstorm creative ways to bridge the gap between the Current State and the Ideal State.
8. Evaluate the ideas and select the best one by consensus.
9. Decide what steps and what resources are necessary to achieve this objective; that is, develop an action plan.
10. Decide on a process and milestones for reviewing progress and making mid-course corrections.

# Appendix H

## Nominal Group Technique

The Nominal Group Technique (NGT) is a very energizing, 10-step, collaborative process for achieving consensus.[33] For example, NGT is a quick way for a team to develop a list of key issues (such as agenda topics or action items) and put them in priority order based on a team consensus.

### Step 1

Each person takes a few minutes to write down what they feel are the key issues. An individual's list may contain as many items as they can write within the allotted time.

### Step 2

Each person reviews their list and designates three items as the highest priority, ranking them 1 (highest), 2, and 3 (lowest) according to their importance to the team's success.

### Step 3

The leader asks each person to state their number 1 priority, and the recorder writes it on a (real or electronic) flip chart or white board. If someone has already mentioned a person's number 1 item, they state their number 2 item; if their number 2 item is already on the list, they state their number 3 item. If all three of their items are on the list, the person passes.

Do not allow anyone to state two or all three priorities at one time. Rather, continue the round-robin process until the recorder has listed everyone's top three priorities.

*Step 4*

The recorder gives a sequential number to each of the items.

*Step 5*

The group discusses each item, clarifying its meaning.

*Step 6*

The group reviews the list, eliminating duplicates. Wherever possible, combine related items into one. Be sure to ask the originators of ideas for their permission before eliminating or consolidating items. If an originator does not agree that two items are essentially the same, the group must treat them as separate items.

*Step 7*

Each group member votes on the three highest-priority items. If the list is particularly long, allow people to vote for the top-five items. Each person gets three votes (or five when voting for the top five). No one can assign more than one vote to a single item.

There are two ways to vote. In a large or virtual group, go down the list of items, asking the group to vote for each by a show of hands. With a small group, have everybody specify their votes for the top-priority items individually.

*Step 8*

The recorder creates a table, listing the top vote getters, the item numbers of each, the number of votes received, and a brief description of the item. The table might look something like this:

| Priority | Item | Votes | Description |
|----------|------|-------|-------------|
| 1 | 12 | 18 | RESOURCE ALLOCATION |
| 2 | 2 | 15 | BUDGET OVERRUNS |
| 3 | 5 | 10 | LACK OF TEAMWORK |
| 4 | 8 | 7 | POOR COMMUNICATION |

*Step 9*

The top-priority issues on this list are the team's consensus of the tasks they should focus on.

*Step 10*

Periodically the team reviews their priorities, adjusting them to reflect completed tasks and incorporate new issues.

# Appendix I

## Applying the UMR Model

In Chapter 6, you learned about Lewin's UMR model of change—Unfreezing, Moving, and Refreezing. In this appendix, we apply the model to a common organizational problem, resistance to change.

To enable the unfreezing stage, use Force Field Analysis to list, prioritize, and examine two types of forces for change, those that enable the change and those that hinder it. This table contains a hypothetical list of key forces for the problem of resistance to change:

| Enabling Forces | Hindering Forces |
|---|---|
| Strong Need to Change | Significant Uncertainty |
| Committed People | Poor Communication |
| Strong Leadership | High Rate of Change |
| Stakeholder Support | Fear of Failure |

Confronted with this formidable set of enabling and hindering forces, what is the best way to proceed? Do you increase the enabling forces, decrease the hindering forces, or do some combination of both?

Many leaders, when they sense resistance to change, react by increasing the strength of the enabling forces. In sharp contrast, experts in change management using Kurt Lewin's UMR model (see Chapter 6) encourage leaders to respond by reducing the strength of the hindering forces. The former approach generally results in an increase in the hindering forces, whereas the latter reduces the hindering forces by addressing the root causes of the problem.

The principal strategy for reducing the hindering forces is to create a collective agreement on the need to change and a captivating, common vision of the future by engaging in active, two-way communication and problem solving with stakeholders. Explaining the need for change in a non-threatening manner and engaging people in a dialogue about what they need to do to address the problem will effectively unfreeze the situation in most cases.

The moving step in the UMR model occurs as a result of implementing the decisions made from analyzing the issues identified in the initial, unfreezing step using one or more of the collaborative problem-solving and decision-making methods described earlier in Chapter 5. The participative implementation processes discussed in Chapter 6 facilitate the adoption of the necessary change.

As described in Chapter 7, the refreezing step in the UMR model involves institutionalizing the changes, monitoring their effect, and making any necessary adjustments based on the team and organizational learning that occurs.

# Appendix J

## The Perfect Team Model FAQ

**Does the process for building the perfect team apply to face-to-face and virtual teams?**

Yes. Teams are people, not machines. So, applying the Perfect Team Model is a people process, whether the team meets face-to-face or virtually. Think of technology as a tool to facilitate team meetings, not something that differentiates one way of meeting from another.

**Is building the perfect team a linear process?**

No. The model has seven steps that guide the team leader (or the team itself for autonomous teams), but implementing those steps is an iterative (trial-and-error) process that differs for every team.

**Is it worth the effort?**

Yes. The potential benefits far outweigh the risks. Higher team performance and satisfaction, greater stakeholder engagement in the change process, an improved rate of project success, and enhanced organizational learning and performance are reasons for making a major effort to build perfect teams.

# Notes

1. Robert E. Levasseur, "People Skills: Ensuring Project Success—A Change Management Perspective." *Interfaces* 40, no. 2 (March–April 2010).
2. Charles Duhigg, "What Google Learned From Its Quest to Build the Perfect Team," *New York Times*, February 25, 2016.
3. Otto Kroeger and Janet M. Thuesen, *Type Talk* (New York: Delacorte, 1988).
4. Edgar H. Schein, *Organizational Culture and Leadership* (San Francisco: Jossey-Bass, 2004).
5. Robert E. Levasseur, "People Skills: Marketing OR/MS—A People Problem." *Interfaces* 37, no. 4 (July–August 2007), 383.
6. Duhigg, "What Google Learned."
7. Gallup, "State of the American Workplace," 2017. See https://www.gallup.com/workplace/285818/state-american-workplace-report.aspx
8. Robert E. Levasseur, *Breakthrough Business Meetings: Shared Leadership in Action* (St. Augustine, FL: MindFire Press, 2019), 81-85.
9. Robert E. Levasseur, "People Skills: Optimizing Team Development and Performance." *Interfaces* 41, no. 2 (March–April 2011).
10. Robert E. Levasseur, "People Skills: Change Management Tools—Leading Teams." *Interfaces* 35, no. 2 (March–April 2005).
11. David W. Johnson and Roger T. Johnson. *Cooperation and Competition: Theory and Research* (Edina, MN: Interaction Book Company, 1989).
12. James M. Burns. *Leadership* (New York: Perennial, 1978), 1-5.

13. David L. Bradford and Allan R. Cohen. *Managing for Excellence: The Guide to Developing High Performance in Contemporary Organizations* (New York: John Wiley and Sons, 1984).

14. Robert E. Levasseur, "People Skills: Change Management Tools—The Modern Leadership Model." *Interfaces* 34, no. 2 (March–April 2004).

15. Bradford and Cohen, *Managing for Excellence.*

16. Levasseur, "Leading Teams."

17. Levasseur, *Breakthrough Business Meetings*, 41-44.

18. Robert E. Levasseur, "People Skills: Change Management Tools—Ideal State Analysis." *Interfaces* 32, no. 4 (July–August 2004).

19. Wyatt W. Burke. *Organization Development: A Normative View* (Reading, MA: Addison-Wesley, 1987).

20. Alfred J. Marrow, *The Practical Theorist: The Life and Work of Kurt Lewin* (New York: Basic Books, 1969), ix.

21. Robert E. Levasseur, "People Skills: Change Management Tools—Lewin's Change Model." *Interfaces* 31, no. 4 (July–August 2001).

22. Bernard M. Bass, "From Transactional to Transformational Leadership: Learning to Share the Vision." *Organizational Dynamics* 18, no. 3 (Winter 1990).

23. Robert E. Levasseur, *Leadership and Change in the 21st Century: A Synthesis of Modern Theory, Research, and Practice* (St. Augustine, FL: MindFire Press, 2006).

24. Robert E. Levasseur, "People Skills: Ensuring Project Success—A Change Management Perspective." *Interfaces* 40, no. 2 (March–April 2010).

25. Burke, *Organization Development*, 54.

26. Peter M. Senge, *The Fifth Discipline* (New York: Doubleday, 1990).

27. Kurt Lewin, *Field Theory in Social Science* (New York: Harper and Row, 1951).

28. Robert E. Levasseur, "People Skills: Building the Perfect Team—A Change Management Perspective." *Interfaces* 47, no. 3 (May–June 2017).

29. Levasseur, *Breakthrough Business Meetings*, 81-93.

30. Ibid., 67-72.

31. Ibid., 72-74.

32. Ibid., 74-80.

33. Ibid., 27-30.

# About the Author

Robert E. Levasseur, Ph.D., a faculty member at several of America's premier online Ph.D. granting universities, teaches doctoral courses and serves on the dissertation committees of students of management and public policy and administration. To date, Dr. Levasseur has worked with over 100 students to help them achieve their goal of earning a doctorate. His research interests include leadership and organizational change, the application of quantitative methods to decision making, high-performance team development, collaborative meeting management, and organization development and change management. Dr. Levasseur, a Maine native, earned undergraduate degrees in physics and electrical engineering from Bowdoin College and MIT, and master's degrees in electrical engineering and management from Northeastern University and the MIT Sloan School of Management, respectively. His Ph.D. in Applied Management and Decision Sciences is from Walden University.

Dr. Levasseur has taught part time for Boston University, Franklin University, the International School of Management, Northcentral University, and the University of Maryland University College, and full-time for the University of the Virgin Islands and Walden University. Dr. Levasseur's professional career spanned over three decades, and included positions in leadership, management, and organizational change in Fortune 50 corporations. He is a charter member of the Institute for Operations Research and the Management Sciences (INFORMS) and a Registered Organization Development Consultant. Dr. Levasseur is the author of numerous books and journal articles.

# Books by Robert E. Levasseur

### *Breakthrough Business Meetings*

Professor Edgar Schein of the MIT Sloan School of Management said that *Breakthrough Business Meetings* is "one of the most theoretically sound yet totally practical books on meetings and group management that I have ever read."

### *Leadership and Change in the 21st Century*

Written for the student, scholar, and thoughtful practitioner, *Leadership and Change in the 21st Century* contains theoretical and practical insights that every modern leader needs to know to tackle the important problems of the 21st century.

### *Student to Scholar*

*Student to Scholar* is a must if you are currently a doctoral student or expect to be one soon, and you want to get the most out of the time, money, and effort you invest in your doctoral program.

### *Dissertation Research: An Integrative Approach*

Written by a university professor who has worked with over 100 students to help them achieve their goal of earning a doctorate, this book contains practical information about what to do at each stage of the dissertation process and why to do it, as well as specific examples of how to do it.

## *Practical Statistics*

Written in non-mathematical terms for anyone who wants to learn basic statistics for work, school, research, or the sheer enjoyment of gaining new knowledge, *Practical Statistics* focuses on the practical application of statistics to decision making.

To learn more about these books, visit Dr. L's website at https://robertelevasseurphd.com. Contact him by email at DrL@mindfirepress.com.

www.ingramcontent.com/pod-product-compliance
Lightning Source LLC
Chambersburg PA
CBHW031951190326
41519CB00007B/758